# WHAT DO SHARKS EAT FOR DINNER?

## Questions and Answers About Sharks

BY MELVIN AND GILDA BERGER
ILLUSTRATED BY JOHN RICE

SCHOLASTIC REFERENCE

# CONTENTS

**KEY TO ABBREVIATIONS**

cm = centimeter/centimetre
kg = kilogram
km = kilometer/kilometre
kph = kilometers/kilometres per hour
m  = meter/metre
t = tonne

*Library of Congress Cataloging-in-Publication Data*

Berger, Melvin.
    What do sharks eat for dinner?: questions and answers about sharks / by Melvin and Gilda Berger; illustrated by John Rice.]
    p.    cm. — (Scholastic question and answer series)
    Includes index. Summary: Uses a question-and-answer format to provide information about the physical characteristics, habits, and behavior of sharks.
    1. Sharks—Miscellanea—Juvenile literature. [1. Sharks—Miscellanea. 2. Questions and answers.] I. Berger, Gilda. II. Rice, John, 1958– ill. III. Title.
QL638.9 .B474 2000      597.3—dc21      99-059899      CIP      AC

ISBN  0-439-22905-7

*Book design by David Saylor and Nancy Sabato*

10 9 8 7 6 5 4 3 2      01 02 03 04

Printed in the U.S.A.      08
First trade printing, September 2001

Expert Reader: Lisa Mielke, Assistant Director of Education, New York Aquarium, Brooklyn, NY

*The sharks on the cover are great white sharks. On the title page, there are mako sharks and pilot fish. The shark on page 3 is a small spotted catshark.*

For the boys and girls of the Jefferson School and their remarkable principal, Jane Hyman
— M. AND G. BERGER

To my father... I'll always cherish those wonderful summer days spent fishing with Dad!
— J. RICE

# INTRODUCTION

Most experts believe that sharks have been on Earth for about 350 million years. That means they were here before the dinosaurs—and they're still here.

Why have sharks survived for so long?

One reason is that sharks are particularly well adapted to their environment. Sharks can eat just about anything that lives in the water. They are also equipped with keen senses to locate their prey, and sharp teeth and powerful jaws to nab their victims. Shark skeletons are made up of cartilage—like the tip of your nose and your ears—which is flexible enough to twist and turn as a shark chases its prey. And most kinds of sharks have a streamlined shape that helps them move smoothly through water, causing the least amount of drag to slow them down.

For millions of years, sharks had few enemies except for larger sharks, dolphins, and a few kinds of whales. Then, things began to change. Humans started hunting sharks for food and for other reasons. In recent years, the number of sharks people have caught and killed has increased sharply. Shark fishing has become a popular business and a favorite form of recreation.

As a result of the senseless killing, some kinds of sharks are now scarce and in danger of becoming extinct. Since sharks are at the top of the ocean food chain, their disappearance threatens to upset the balance of nature. Learning about sharks is a first step in helping to save them. It's time to appreciate and admire sharks, and to stop killing them.

# HUNGRY SHARKS

## What do sharks eat for dinner?

Anything they want! Sharks eat just about every creature found in the sea—including other sharks. Big sharks eat smaller sharks, which eat even smaller sharks, and so on down the line.

When they're not eating one another, sharks prey on all kinds of fish and shellfish. Large sharks also make meals of big sea animals, such as seals, dolphins, and sea lions.

## Are sharks always hungry?

No. Yet some sharks do eat huge amounts of food at one time. Certain sharks, such as the great white, never seem to fill up. Sometimes they'll finish eating a large sea animal, and minutes later, find another animal that they gulp down, too. These sharks seem to be hunting and eating all the time.

Most sharks, however, eat only one big meal every two or three days. When food is scarce, they can go weeks without eating. Luckily, sharks, like most animals and humans, store digested food as fat in their bodies to help them survive in hard times.

## Do sharks eat dead animals?

Yes. Sharks also frequently prey on animals that are sick, injured, or old. Such animals, as you can imagine, are easier to capture than young and healthy prey.

Feeding on animals that have trouble escaping or fighting back provides sharks with the food they need. It also helps to keep the oceans clean. And weeding out weak animals makes it easier for those that live to find food and thrive.

Tiger shark

Great white shark

## How can a shark bite with its mouth on the underside of its head?

Easily. The shark tilts its head up and back. Then, as it opens its mouth, the jaws move apart and forward. CHOMP! The lower teeth stab the prey. The upper jaw comes down hard with a powerful, cutting bite.

## How many teeth do sharks have?

Plenty! Some have as many as 3,000. Others have only a few dozen. However, a shark's teeth are not in one row like yours. They form several rows, one behind the other.

When a shark bites, its front teeth may fall out or break off. In about a day or two, new teeth from behind move forward to take their place, much like the steps of an escalator moving up and ahead. These new teeth now stand sharp and ready to bite.

## Why do sharks' teeth fall out?

Because they're not firmly attached to the jaw like yours and are easily knocked loose. A single shark can grow—and lose—as many as 20,000 teeth in its lifetime. A shark tooth fairy would quickly go broke!

## Do all shark teeth have the same shape?

No. The shape depends on the shark and its diet. The great white shark has teeth shaped like little triangles, with jagged, sawlike edges perfect for ripping through the tough skins of large tunas and sea mammals.

A sand tiger shark, which eats smaller fish and squid, has fanglike teeth with thin, sharp tips to catch and hold on to these slippery creatures.

The solid, flat teeth of a nurse shark form powerful grinders that crush the shells of crabs, clams, and lobsters to let the shark reach the meat inside.

## Which sharks have the biggest teeth for their size?

Cookiecutter sharks. Even though they are some of the smallest sharks, this species has larger teeth for its size than any other kind of shark. These sharks hunt for tunas, whales, dolphins, and other sharks, and use their teeth like cookie cutters to cut out circles of flesh.

Believe it or not, giant-sized whale sharks have among the *smallest* teeth for their size. Fortunately, they do not need their teeth for eating. They strain the tiny animals and plants, called plankton, and the fish they feed on from the water.

## Do sharks chew their food?

No. Sharks use their teeth to capture and hold their prey, not to chew them. If the prey are small, sharks swallow them whole. For larger victims, the sharks bite off chunks of flesh and gulp them down piece by piece.

Megamouth shark

Remora

## Do all sharks bite their prey?

No. Some large sharks, such as the whale shark, basking shark, and megamouth shark, strain their food out of the water.

These sharks swim along with their mouths open, taking in tremendous amounts of water. In the water are billions of plankton. Big, comblike strainers in the sharks' gills trap the plankton and the sharks gulp them down. The water flows out through gill slits in the animals' sides.

To keep their gigantic bellies filled, whale sharks take in almost 2,000 tons (2,032 t) of water *every hour*!

## How strong are a shark's jaws?

Very strong. A shark's jaws are about twice as powerful as the jaws of a lion. Scientists tell us that the strongest shark bite ever recorded measured 132 pounds (60 kg) of force per tooth. With strength like that, a shark can bite through steel.

## Do sharks hunt in packs?

Some do. For example, groups of green dogfish sharks, which are small, often hunt far larger octopuses and squids. When attacking, the dogfish swim around the prey, each shark ripping out chunks of flesh with its sharp teeth.

Several threshers, sandbar sharks, or spiny dogfish sometimes gather a whole school of fish, like shepherds herding a flock of sheep. Once the fish are crowded together, the sharks swim in and gulp mouthfuls of them at a time.

Whale sharks and basking sharks occasionally cluster in groups of 20 or more to feed where there are lots of plankton.

## What is a feeding frenzy?

A group of out-of-control sharks. A feeding frenzy often starts when one or two sharks detect a large injured fish in the water. Attracted by the smell of blood, the sharks rush in to attack.

As more blood flows into the water, other sharks pick up the scent and speed over. Soon all the sharks are slashing away at the struggling victim—and sometimes even at one another. Their whirling, thrashing bodies turn the foaming water red with blood— which draws even more sharks.

Feeding frenzies last for just a few minutes. Then, suddenly, it's all over. The survivors silently glide away. Only bloody water and floating scraps of flesh remain.

Gray reef sharks

Great hammerhead sharks

Southern stingray

## Which sense helps a shark most?

Hearing. When hunting, a shark's sharp hearing provides the first clue that dinner is at hand—especially when the prey is far away. Sound vibrations travel about five times faster in water than in air, so a good sense of hearing is vitally important for locating food. Sound also travels farther in water. A shark can sense a fish thrashing about in the water more than ½ mile (0.8 km) away!

## Where are a shark's ears?

Behind its eyes. Shark ears don't look anything like your ears or the ears of most land mammals. They consist of two tiny, nearly invisible holes in the skin just behind the shark's eyes. Sound vibrations enter the inner ear and are changed to electrical signals going to the brain, which helps the shark figure out the source of a sound.

## Do sharks have nostrils like yours?

Yes. But the shark's nostrils are just for sniffing, not for sniffing and breathing like your nostrils.

And what good sniffers sharks are. They can smell as little as one very tiny drop of blood in a huge tank of water! Small wonder—about two-thirds of a shark's brain is devoted to its sense of smell.

## Why do swimming sharks sometimes swing their heads from side to side?

To follow a smell. While swimming through the water, sharks pick up various scents. By swinging their heads, they find the direction from which the odor is strongest and follow it closer and closer to the source of the smell.

# Which shark is built best for smelling?

The hammerhead shark. This big shark sweeps its broad, hammer-shaped head from side to side to pick up smells in the water. Widely separated nostrils at either end of the bar on its head make it especially easy for a hammerhead to track down smells. Its sense of smell is helped by tiny openings in the skin that allow the shark to pick up weak electrical signals given off by its prey.

Stingrays, a favorite food of hammerheads, often lie buried in the sandy ocean bottom. But few can escape a hunting hammerhead with its sharp sense of smell. Quick as a shot, the shark sniffs out the stingray and swallows it—poisonous tail and all!

# Do sharks see well?

Yes, from short distances. Sharks depend on their sense of sight to help them close in on their prey and attack.

Sharks that live in deeper water tend to have bigger eyes than sharks that live closer to the surface. The reason is simple. Bigger eyes can collect more of the dim light that reaches the lower parts of the sea. The deep-sea thresher shark, for example, has some of the biggest eyes. They are the size of human fists.

# How are sharks like cats?

Both see well in the dark. Sharks and cats have the same mirrorlike structure in the back of the eye, called a tapetum (tuh-PEE-tum). The tapetum reflects, or bounces back, light into the eye, making it easier for the animals to see in dim light.

If you shine a light into a cat's eyes at night, its eyes will appear to glow greenish or silvery as the light is reflected off them. But don't try it with a shark!

## Do sharks have a sense of touch?

Yes. A shark feels close objects with its skin just as you do. A shark's skin, like that of all other fish, is covered with scales. But most fish scales are smooth. A shark's scales are rough and sharp. They are actually small, jagged teeth!

A shark senses more distant objects with an organ called the lateral line. This line runs along each side of the shark's body, from head to tail. In some sharks, the lateral line looks like a raised stripe. Tiny jelly-filled tubes, which extend out from the lateral line through very small holes in the skin, pick up the slightest change in water pressure caused by fish or other objects. And, lightning fast, the tubes pass the signals to the shark's brain.

Lateral line

Lemon shark

Scales

Gray reef
sharks

Pilot fish

Remoras

Nurse shark

## Can a shark taste?

Definitely. A shark has tiny taste buds that dot the inside of its mouth and throat. As it bites its prey, the shark's taste buds let it know whether the food is good enough to swallow.

Some bottom-dwelling sharks have an added way of tasting. Two or more fleshy feelers, called barbels, hang around their heads and let them taste the food *before* they eat it.

## Do sharks have a sixth sense?

Yes, an electrical sense. Sharks have about 1,500 tiny pores, or holes, around their heads and snouts that pick up weak electrical signals in the water. Some of the signals come from the animals sharks prey on, including those that hide on the ocean bottom or in underwater reefs or caves.

All animals—land *and* sea—give off tiny electrical signals. Sharks can sense very weak electrical signals at short distances. Some say that a shark can detect the electricity from a small battery at a distance of 1 mile (1.6 km)!

## Why don't sharks eat pilot fish?

No one knows. Small pilot fish swim around large sharks in complete safety. People used to think the pilot fish were not in danger because they helped lead sharks toward prey. Experts no longer believe that this is true, but the fish keep their name.

## Which fish hitchhike on sharks?

Remoras, or sucker fish. They attach themselves to sharks with large suction plates on the tops of their heads. Wherever the sharks go, the remoras go, too. These fish probably help the shark stay healthy by eating parasites and small shellfish that dig into the shark's skin. Remoras seem to earn the free ride they get.

The remora hangs on with a powerful grip. One scientist tried to pull a remora off a shark. The suction plate ripped off from the remora's head—but stayed attached to the shark!

## Are sharks good swimmers?

Yes. Sharks have a streamlined shape and a powerful tail fin that swings from side to side to move themselves through the water. Large pectoral, or chest, fins help them steer. Fins on their backs, called dorsal fins, and on their undersides, called pelvic and anal fins, keep them from rolling over in the water.

Most sharks cruise along at a speed of about 2 to 3 miles an hour (3 to 5 kph). But when they are closing in on their prey they can reach speeds of more than 40 miles an hour (64 kph). The blue shark, an especially fast swimmer, has been clocked at an amazing 43 miles an hour (69 kph)!

## How are sharks able to twist and turn in the water?

They don't have a single bone in their body! Instead of stiff bones, like most other fish, the shark's skeleton is made of cartilage, a tough, rubbery material that bends easily. Cartilage is the same material that forms your ears and the end of your nose.

## What happens when sharks stop swimming?

They sink to the bottom. Sharks weigh more than water. And like anything heavier than water, they don't float. So, sharks must keep swimming and moving all the time, or down they go.

## What else helps sharks stay afloat?

Their pectoral fins, which are shaped like airplane wings. Just as airplane wings hold a moving plane up in the air, pectoral fins raise a swimming shark in the water. Also, its body shape, curved on top and flatter on the bottom, helps keep a shark afloat. Since cartilage weighs much less than bone, sharks have the advantage of a lightweight skeleton.

And finally, a shark's huge liver is filled with oil, which is lighter than water. Large quantities of liver oil give swimming sharks an extra lift.

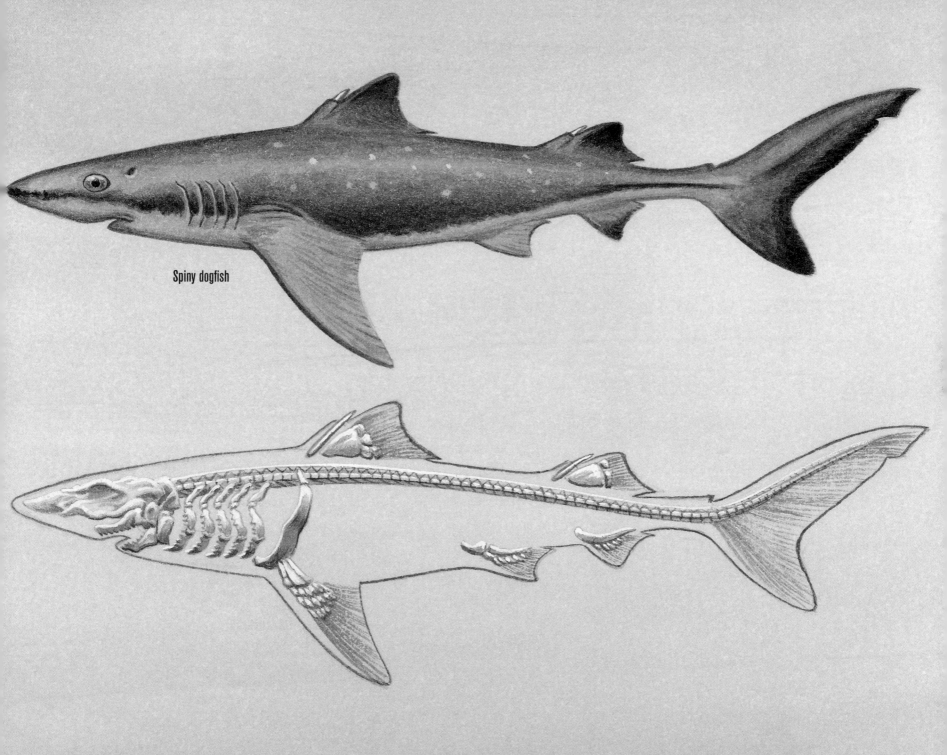

Spiny dogfish

# THE WORLD OF SHARKS

## How long have sharks been on Earth?

About 350 million years! Sharks are among the oldest creatures with skeletons on Earth. They are far older than humans, who have been around for fewer than five million years. Sharks are even older than dinosaurs, which date back only 225 million years. Perhaps most remarkable is the fact that some of today's sharks look very much like the sharks of millions of years ago.

## Have any shark fossils been found?

Yes, a few. But complete shark fossils are few and far between because a shark's cartilage skeleton is softer than bone and decays more quickly.

Much of what we know about ancient sharks comes from fossilized teeth that have survived through the ages. The teeth reveal much about the size, shape, age, and diet of sharks that lived long ago. Since even ancient sharks lost many teeth, scientists find a lot to study.

Frilled shark

# Which modern shark is called a living fossil?

The frilled shark. This rarely seen shark resembles the earliest known sharks in at least two ways. Its mouth is at the front of its head instead of on the underside as in most modern sharks. Also, the frilled shark has about 26 teeth in each of its 20 rows of teeth, as compared to today's toothier sharks.

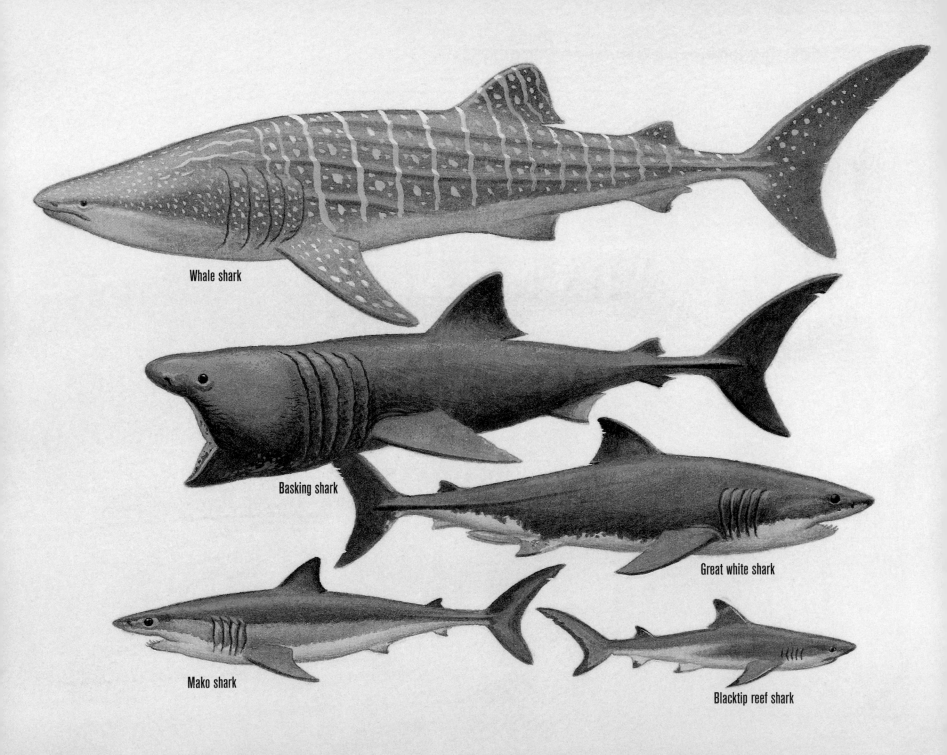

Whale shark

Basking shark

Great white shark

Mako shark

Blacktip reef shark

# How many kinds of sharks are there today?

About 370. Most typical are the torpedo-shaped sharks, such as blue or sand tiger sharks. They average about 7 feet (2 m) in length and weigh about 250 pounds (113 kg).

# Which unusual shark was discovered most recently?

The megamouth shark. In 1976, sailors on a United States Navy ship sailing near Hawaii hauled up the anchor and found a live 15-foot-long (5 m) shark entangled in the chain. No one had ever seen a shark like this. Most striking was the shark's gigantic mouth and the 1,000 teeth in its lower jaw. On the spot, the sailors dubbed it megamouth, or "big mouth." Since then, about seven more megamouths have been found in tropical seas.

# Which is the smallest shark?

The dwarf shark. Each is no longer than about 6 inches (15 cm), so you could easily hold one in the palm of your hand. But on second thought—would you really want to?

# Which is the largest shark?

The whale shark. At more than 60 feet (18 m) in length and about 13 tons (13.2 t) in weight, the whale shark is also the largest of all fish. Imagine a fish the size of a trailer truck!

# Which kind of shark is the most numerous?

The oceanic whitetip. Huge numbers of whitetips swim in the warm waters of both the Atlantic and Pacific oceans. They take their name from the white markings on their fins and tail.

Among the smaller sharks, the spiny dogfish shark is most numerous. Millions swim along rocky coasts in the North Atlantic Ocean.

# How are sharks born?

Most baby sharks, called pups, are born live from eggs that grow inside the mother's body. Mother sharks give birth to large, strong pups that have teeth and know how to swim. From the moment they leave their mother's body, the young sharks start hunting.

Some kinds of female sharks lay eggs in egg cases that they deposit in shallow, sheltered waters. When the eggs hatch, the pups wiggle out and are on their own, hunting worms, shellfish, and small fish in the water.

People sometimes find empty shark egg cases on beaches. They are called mermaids' purses.

# How many pups are born at a time?

From 2 to 40. Most kinds of sharks give birth to fewer than 10 pups at once.

# Do sharks care for their young?

No. The parents neither care for nor protect the young. After the mother gives birth, she swims away, leaving her pups to make their own way in the water.

Lemon shark pup

24

## Do all the pups survive?

Rarely. Sometimes, the first pups to be born eat the other pups. This is a normal, natural part of shark behavior. Also, the mother occasionally eats her own offspring after they leave the area where they were born.

## Do pups look like their parents?

Usually they do. But shark pups may be slimmer and more snakelike in shape than adult sharks. As the pups grow, their skin color fades, which may allow them to hide better in the water. They also get larger teeth so they can feed on bigger and bigger prey.

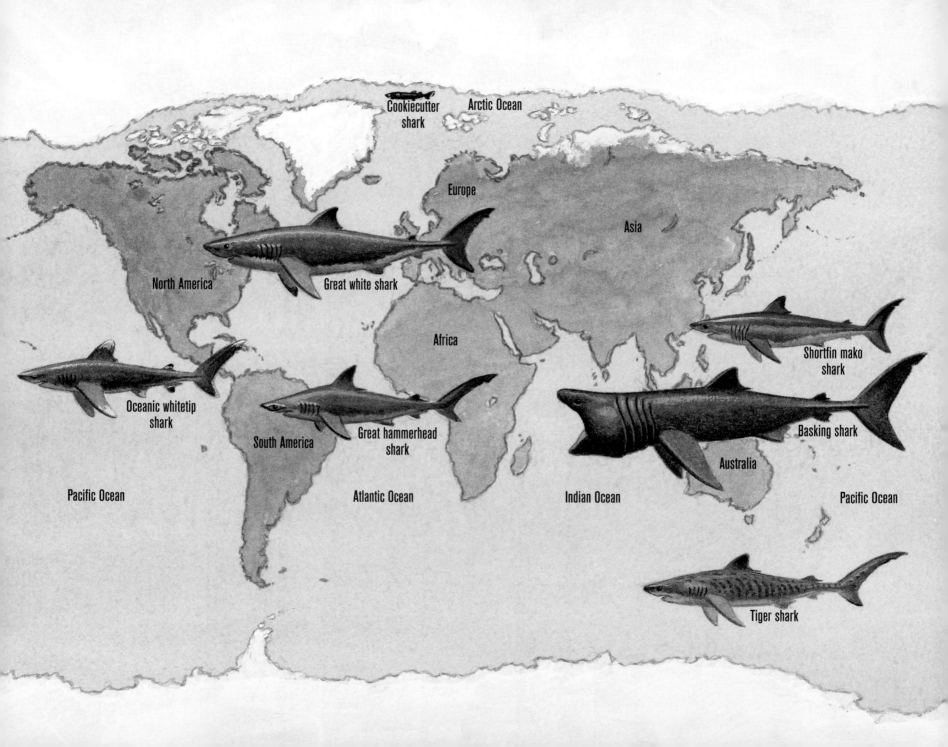

Cookiecutter shark

Arctic Ocean

Europe

Asia

North America

Great white shark

Africa

Shortfin mako shark

Oceanic whitetip shark

South America

Great hammerhead shark

Basking shark

Australia

Pacific Ocean

Atlantic Ocean

Indian Ocean

Pacific Ocean

Tiger shark

## Why did ancient people invent legends about sharks?

To calm their fears. For example, long ago, people on the Hawaiian islands invented a helpful god that they called Kama-Hoa-Lii, "the king of all sharks." The people believed that Kama-Hoa-Lii was a giant shark that lived in an immense cavern in the waters near Honolulu and protected fishermen. If a crew of a boat needed help in a storm, or if someone got hurt, the men lit a fire and poured juice from the *awa* plant into the sea. They believed Kama-Hoa-Lii would receive their appeal and send some of his sharks to rescue the endangered fishermen.

## Where do sharks live?

In every ocean of the world. Some sharks swim only in the deepest parts of the ocean. They dive down as far as 2 miles (3 km) below the surface. Others are usually found in shallow water along sandy or rocky coasts. These sharks may swim so close to the surface that you can see their fins sticking up above the water.

Most sharks spend their time in warm waters. But sharks also live in temperate and polar oceans.

## Why do more sharks live in warm waters?

Because they are cold-blooded. This means that a shark's body is about the same temperature as the water in which it swims. In warm water, sharks have enough energy to swim fast and catch their prey. In cold water, sharks slow down and can't hunt as well.

## What do sharks do in winter?

Some migrate. Migrating sharks move toward the equator when the weather starts to grow cold. When the season changes and the waters near the equator get too warm, the sharks return home.

## Do sharks breathe?

Yes. Sharks breathe oxygen from the water, just as you breathe oxygen from the air. As sharks swim, water enters their mouths and flows over sheets of tissue called gills. The gills collect oxygen from the water. Blood in the gills then carries the oxygen around the body. The water flows out through gill slits just behind the shark's head.

## Does water contain as much oxygen as air?

Not by a long shot! About 20 percent of air is oxygen. But oxygen makes up only about 1 percent of water.

## Do sharks die if they stop swimming?

Some sharks will. As you know, sharks get the oxygen they need to breathe from water flowing over their gills. When they stop swimming, the flow of water stops, and so does the flow of oxygen. The sharks can't breathe and they suffocate. Some sharks are not able to pump water over their gills like other fish and therefore cannot survive unless they are moving in the water.

Also, if sharks stop swimming, they drift down to the bottom of the sea. Most fish have balloonlike swim bladders in their bodies to keep them afloat in the water. Sharks don't.

## Do any sharks breathe without swimming?

Yes, sharks that live on the ocean bottom, such as carpet, nurse, and angel sharks. Water flows in through holes near their eyes and sometimes through their mouths. Muscles pass the water over the gills and push it out through the gill slits, which lets these sharks rest and breathe at the same time.

Port Jackson shark

Gills

Porbeagle shark

## Do sharks make sounds?

A few do. Whale sharks croak and grunt; wobbegongs, which live near Australia, make gruff sounds as they grip their prey; and swell sharks have been heard barking. But scientists do not believe these sounds are used for communication.

Sharks communicate in other ways. Some release substances into the water that other sharks can smell. At mating time, for example, male sharks discharge chemicals into the water that attract female sharks. And sharks use their posture—especially a threatening posture—to send signals to other creatures.

## Do sharks play?

Perhaps. But most likely it only looks like play to us. Sharks examine their food carefully to see if it can be eaten. Great white sharks sometimes nudge and taste objects they find floating at the surface. Porbeagle sharks, too, often inspect drifting debris or seaweed.

Every once in a while, the objects that sharks investigate are live animals, such as penguins. They usually don't get eaten, but imagine their fright!

Sometimes two great white sharks scuffle over a seal or other large animal. The two sharks splash the water with their tail fins. The one who slaps the water harder and faster usually gets the seal for dinner.

## Can sharks learn?

Yes. Recent studies show that sharks can remember and learn from experience. In one experiment, sharks in tanks learned to take food from their trainers. In another, the sharks learned to recognize different shapes—a circle meant there was food and a square meant there was none.

# SHARKS AND PEOPLE

## Do sharks attack people?

Occasionally. But people are definitely not part of a shark's diet.

In the entire world, only about 50 people a year are likely to be attacked by sharks. Of these, fewer than 20 will die. Experts say you are more likely to die in an automobile accident, be struck by lightning, or get bitten by a poisonous snake than be killed in a shark attack.

Fewer than 20 percent of all known species of sharks are dangerous to humans. Experts believe that the great white shark, tiger shark, bull shark, and oceanic whitetip shark are the ones that pose the greatest threat.

## What causes shark attacks?

Instinct. A shark is a wild creature hunting for prey. Whenever it sees, smells, hears, or feels something that might be food, it hurries over. A person on a surfboard may look like a seal to a shark that is swimming below.

A swimmer splashing or anyone in the water bleeding from a cut or scrape also attracts sharks. The sharks may charge and bite, sometimes more than once, before swimming away in search of their usual prey.

## Why do sharks sometimes bite, but not eat, humans?

Probably because our bodies contain too little fat. Eating fat provides the shark with twice as much energy as eating other flesh. So, sharks prefer fattier animals, such as seals and sea lions, to leaner animals, like humans, which they usually spit out.

# How can you avoid a shark attack?

Follow the rules.

1. Don't swim in water that may have sharks in it.
2. Always swim with a buddy.
3. Do not go into the water if you are bleeding from a cut or scrape.
4. Swim in clear water so you can see danger.
5. If someone sees a shark, leave the water, trying not to splash.
6. Don't touch small or injured sharks; they may still be able to bite you.
7. When fishing, don't put your hand in the water. Sharks may be attracted to fish in your net or at the end of your line.

## Which is the most-feared shark?

The great white shark. About 15 feet (5 m) long and 1,400 pounds (635 kg) in weight, the great white is the biggest of all meat-eating sharks.

Because of its size, the great white tends to go after large prey, such as seals and sea lions. Many great white shark attacks on humans seem to occur because the shark mistakes the swimmer or surfer for a large sea animal. But no swimmer or surfer would ever mistake the great white, with its big, black, unblinking eyes and its slightly open mouth, for anything else in the world.

## What makes the great white shark a perfect predator?

Its many rows of very sharp teeth—each up to 2 inches (5 cm) long. The very narrow and pointed teeth in the lower jaw are like forks for holding food. The sharp, jagged top teeth are like the sharpest knives and are used for biting food.

Great whites are nearly always ready to eat. In one year, a single great white consumes about 11 tons (11.2 t) of food. Compare this with an adult human who weighs only about one-tenth as much as a great white shark, but eats less than one-twentieth as much food.

## Are great white sharks really white?

No, they're gray. Light gray bellies make great white sharks hard to see from underneath; they look as light as the sky above them. A darker gray on their backs makes them hard to see from above; they blend in with the darker water.

## Where are most great white sharks found?

In all oceans, but mostly in deep waters that are cool or temperate. When the temperature drops very low, great whites migrate to warmer waters.

Great white shark

## Are there lots of great white sharks in the sea?

No. In fact, there are very few. Some scientists believe the total number in the entire world is fewer than 10,000! Australia recently placed the great white shark on its list of endangered animals, and South Africa and the state of California passed laws protecting these sharks.

Tiger sharks

## Which shark is called a swimming garbage can?

The tiger shark, because it will eat anything. From the stomach of a tiger shark caught off the coast of Australia, one fisherman pulled out the remains of a goat, a turtle, a cat, three birds, many fish, and a 6-foot-long (2 m) shark! Another tiger shark caught in the Philippines had nine shoes, a belt, and a pair of trousers in its belly. Other tiger sharks have yielded glass bottles, rolls of wire, and an oil drum that weighed 18 pounds (8 kg)!

## Why are people afraid of tiger sharks?

Because they swim in shallow ocean waters along with human swimmers, surfers, and divers. During the day, tiger sharks are found far from shore. But late in the afternoon, they often move in toward land. Unfortunately, that is when many people are in the water enjoying themselves along beaches or seacoasts.

Sometimes tiger sharks are in such shallow water that their fins stick up above the surface. So, watch out! If you ever see shark fins, get out of the water fast, splashing as little as possible.

## Where did the tiger shark get its name?

From the brown, tigerlike stripes on the bodies of young tiger sharks. As the shark grows older, though, the stripes fade in color, but its name stays the same.

## How are bull sharks like tiger sharks?

They are both very dangerous because they swim in shallow water. Bull sharks are heavier than tiger sharks and have short, rounded snouts and small, staring eyes. Most of the time, these sharks swim slowly and sluggishly along rocky or sandy seacoasts. But when they are chasing prey, they can put on amazing bursts of speed.

From time to time, bull sharks leave the sea and stray into rivers or lakes. Some have wandered into streams in Florida and Louisiana and up the Mississippi River. Others are sometimes found in smaller bodies of water in South and Central America, Africa, and India.

# Which sharks are a danger in deep-sea waters?

Mako sharks. These fierce, fast-moving sharks are a particular threat to people who survive shipwrecks or plane crashes in the middle of the ocean. Mako sharks swim swiftly and silently, and they strike with startling speed. Eight rows of smooth, long, slender, and very sharp teeth fatally injure most victims.

# How do carpet sharks attack?

By surprise. No one expects trouble from carpet sharks that rest like flat blobs on the ocean floor all day long. But if a swimmer accidentally steps on or kicks a carpet shark, the shark quickly buries several rows of needle-sharp teeth in the victim's leg. And it doesn't let go. Attacking carpet sharks have been shot, pounded on the head, and stabbed without loosening their mighty grip!

# Which deep-sea shark moves like a snake?

The nurse shark. This slow-moving fish lives on the bottom of the sea, often hiding in reefs or underwater caves. When it does move, it slides along the bottom like a snake, hunting shrimps, lobsters, crabs, sea urchins, and other shellfish, crushing their hard shells with its strong, blunt teeth.

Skin divers sometimes forget that the nurse shark is a wild creature. One diver tried to ride a 12-foot-long (4 m) nurse shark. He lost his leg after the shark bit him.

# Is the angel shark really angelic?

Not at all. Its two big, broad pectoral fins may look like the wings of an angel, but that's the only similarity. Like other bottom dwellers, the angel shark is a slow swimmer that often hides on the sandy ocean bottom. It snaps when disturbed.

Some say this completely flat shark looks like a steamroller ran over it, leaving it about 4 feet (1 m) long and 4 feet (1 m) wide across its fins.

Shortfin mako shark

Tasseled
wobbegong

Nurse shark

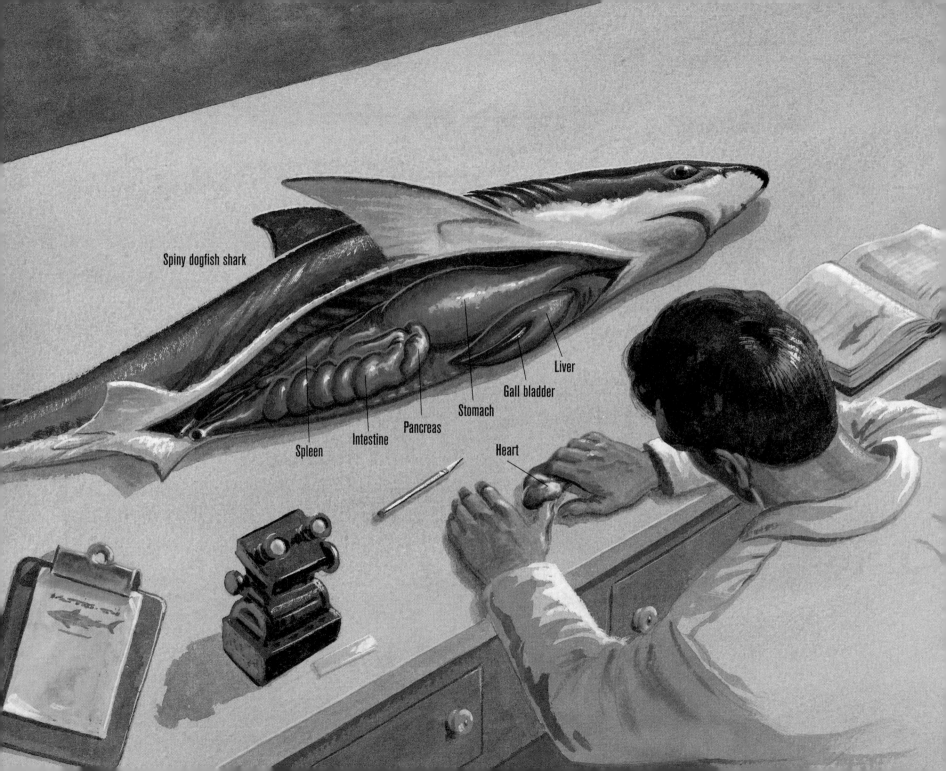

Spiny dogfish shark

Liver

Gall bladder

Stomach

Pancreas

Intestine

Spleen

Heart

## Who are sharks' main enemies?

Humans. People kill millions of sharks every year for their meat, liver oil, cartilage, fins, jaws, and skin.

## Who eats shark meat?

People everywhere. Shark meat is especially popular in Japan and other countries in Asia where diners eat it cooked, dried, and even raw. In England, a favorite dish is fish and chips, which is frequently made with meat from the dogfish shark.

Since some people don't like the idea of eating shark meat, fish markets and chefs often change the name of shark meat to rock salmon, rock eel, huss, or flake.

## What is shark liver oil used for?

To make various products. Until the 1950s, shark liver oil was used to make vitamin A. Today, chemists produce vitamin A in factories. But manufacturers still use shark liver oil to make cosmetics, drugs, lubricants, paints, and candles. The liver from one basking shark, for example, may hold hundreds of gallons (liters) of oil!

## Why do scientists study sharks?

For many reasons. Researchers are studying treatments for humans that use parts of the shark's body. One substance taken from shark's blood may prevent human blood from clotting and may be helpful in treating various diseases. Another material prepared from a shark's liver and stomach may rid the human body of certain kinds of infections. And finally, corneas from shark eyes may be transplanted into humans' eyes to help them see better.

## Do people use sharkskin?

No. Long ago, sharkskin was very popular. Carpenters and jewelers used its rough surface for smoothing and polishing wood and metal. Sword makers covered the handles of their best swords with sharkskin to give them a non-slip grip. And tanners made sharkskin into strong, flexible leather for wallets, belts, jackets, and shoes. Today, people seem to prefer other animal skins to the skin of sharks.

## What food is made from sharks' fins?

Shark-fin soup. Fishermen catch soupfin sharks, also called tope sharks or oil sharks, in large nets or by hook and line. Then they cut off their fins and toss the sharks—often still alive—back into the water. Unable to swim without their fins, many are killed and eaten by other sharks.

To stop this horrible practice, the United States government passed a law in 1993 that forbids catching sharks just for their fins off the Atlantic and Gulf coasts. Yet the killing goes on in other places where the soup is a delicacy.

## How many sharks do humans kill?

Between 30 and 100 million a year! Many sharks are killed for food and other uses. But some people catch sharks just for sport or because they fear or dislike them. Large numbers of sharks die when they are accidentally caught in nets designed to catch tunas, swordfish, or other fish. Some say that fishermen in the Gulf of Mexico kill more than two million sharks a year in nets set out to catch shrimp.

In the last 10 years, the numbers of certain kinds of sharks in the seas have dropped by about 80 percent. Many people fear that sharks may disappear from the seas altogether if we do not work to protect them.

Mako shark

Tuna

Swordfish

## How can we help sharks survive?

We can pass and enforce laws that ban the killing of sharks. In 1999, a special committee of the United Nations voted to create a plan to save the sharks. Around the same time, the United States government cut the number of sharks that could be caught in the waters of the Atlantic Ocean; sport fishermen can catch no more than two sharks per fishing boat. In addition, officials in other nations are preparing laws to protect the sharks.

## Why do we need sharks?

Sharks have much to teach us. Sharks are sleek, graceful, beautiful creatures that play an important part in the chain of life in the sea.

Sharks may hold the key to curing some human diseases.

By eating sick or dying fish, sharks may be slowing the spread of disease among other ocean animals.

And most of all, we have much to learn from sharks. After all, they have been on Earth for more than 350 million years.

Zebra shark

Gray reef sharks

Lemon shark

Necklace carpet shark

# INDEX

## About the Authors

The Bergers find sharks to be curious, exciting, and mysterious creatures, and enjoy writing about them. The authors believe that, because of their long history, sharks have much to teach us about life in the sea.

## About the Illustrator

John Rice says, "Sometimes the things we fear the most are the things we know the least—like the shark." He hopes that through this book, people will learn not to fear sharks, but to see the important and vital role they play in the undersea world.